Ethereum:
A Primer

Your Guide to Understanding, Using, And Profiting from the Digital Currency That's Smarter Than Bitcoin

By

Eric Morse

To those who dare to build upon the shoulders of giants.

This book copyright © 2017 by Eric Morse. All rights reserved. No part of this publication may be reproduced, distributed, or transmitted in any form or by any means, including photocopying, recording, or other electronic or mechanical methods, without the prior written permission of the publisher, except in the case of brief quotations embodied in critical reviews and certain other noncommercial uses permitted by copyright law.

Table of Contents

Introduction 5

Chapter 1: What Is Ethereum 8

Chapter 2: A Short History Lesson 17

Chapter 3: A Currency for the Future 21

Chapter 4: How To Buy Ethereum 30

Chapter 5: How To Use Ethereum 36

Chapter 6: Ethereum Mining 41

Chapter 7: Three Rules 47

Conclusion and Further Reading 52

Introduction

What is Ethereum?

What's so special about it?

You might have been following Bitcoin for some time, but never quite grasped the concept of Ethereum. After all, some alternative cryptocurrencies (or "altcoins") are just clones of Bitcoin, while others appear to be vastly different and much harder to understand. Ethereum seems to fall into the later category... but how, exactly, is it different?

Perhaps you have only heard of Ethereum recently due to its phenomenal price jump in the past few months. You want to know what this investment is, what gives it value, and if there is still any upward potential remaining. In other words: Why are people buying it?

Regardless of what category you're in; your questions will be explained in this book.

Let's start with Bitcoin. You might see it with a lowercase "b" when talking about the currency, or an uppercase B when referring to the payment network on which the currency is used. At its core, Bitcoin is a distributed public ledger called the blockchain, with the associated programming necessary to add and verify transactions. Bitcoin has a scripting language that is used to create transactions that move the bitcoin (note the lowercase) from one person to another. However, there is a shortcoming. While Bitcoin might seem quite complex and powerful, in terms of computer science it has a stunning weakness: it is not Turing-complete. This is just a fancy way of saying that the programming language behind Bitcoin too limited, and thus incapable of performing very complex transactions. In other words: Bitcoin, while powerful, isn't too bright.

Ethereum is the smarter Bitcoin.

The most significant difference between Ethereum and Bitcoin is the purpose and the capability of the two networks. Bitcoin offers a specific blockchain application, that of a peer-to-peer digital cash system. The system allows for online payments of a digital currency that is also called "bitcoin" (abbreviated "BTC"). This network is used for tracking the ownership of the bitcoin currency, but Ethereum is focused on the program code needed to run a decentralized application. To oversimplify it: Bitcoin is all about the blockchain and transactions, while Ethereum focuses on the code. Bitcoin could replace Paypal and Visa. Ethereum could replace insurance companies, venture capital firms, and much of the legal infrastructure that relates to contract law.

Ethereum is a platform upon which other things can be built. Specifically, it is a blockchain-based open-source platform that gives developers the opportunity to build and deploy decentralized applications. Like Bitcoin, it has a distributed public ledger... a blockchain. It also has a currency called "ether" (abbreviated "ETH"). But rather than being spent in the same way as we can make purchases with bitcoin, ether is the fuel that is needed to run programs on Ethereum. Ether can be traded. It has a dollar value. But is generally used by the application developers to pay for the services and the transaction fees on the Ethereum network. You are unlikely to buy a cup of coffee, a car, or a house with ether. But, in the future, your mortgage (or your mortgage company) may be written in code that consumes ether to run on the Ethereum blockchain.

But what does this actually mean in practice? What does Ethereum do with these extra capabilities? More importantly, what can we mere humans do with these capabilities?

Read on...

Chapter 1: What Is Ethereum

Before we launch into our exploration of Ethereum, we need to define some terms and concepts:

Smart Contracts

There's no real difference between a "smart contract" and a normal contract in the traditional sense. They are both agreements that certain parties will perform specific actions under specific circumstances. A Smart Contract is a piece of computer code that contains instructions for a transaction that takes place *only* when certain conditions are met.

All blockchains can process code but most of them are limited in what they can do. That is where Ethereum differs; instead of developers being limited as they are with Bitcoin complexity, they can be built systems of transactions so complex that they can mimic the operation of an entire corporation. More on that later.

You can liken contracts in Ethereum to programmable bank accounts that you can interact with via transactions on the Ethereum network.. While contracts in the real world require the oversight of attorneys or legal professionals to be enacted, in the crypto-world this is not so. This allows for lower expenses, and fewer requirements to be entered into the transaction.

Whenever you sign your name on a sales receipt or click the "I understand" radio button when buying a product or service, you are entering into a contract similar to what you might encounter in Ethereum. However, Ethereum contracts can be enacted by anyone and all users can interact with them in an open manner (similar to simple transaction 'contracts' that move ETH from one person to another). These smart contracts are basically a computer program that has been written in one of the Ethereum high-level programming languages. The primary languages are Solidity or Serpent, but others can be used. Once written, the program is entered into a special transaction along with a minimal transaction fee, payable in Ethereum's currency: ether.

What benefits do smart contracts give us?

Efficiency: In our current legal system, most contracts are written is incredibly complex, yet still open to interpretation. If you and the other party differ on interpretations of a certain contract, the process becomes difficult to thresh out and will likely require court cases or legal mediation. With smart contracts, the contract is written in a logical, almost mathematical way where interpretation is no longer necessary. The question of which party has the correct legal basis is no longer open to discussion or interpretation. Once the contract is deployed into the blockchain, the contract is secured and the execution of the contract will take place in a logical, rational, and mathematical process.

Autonomy: Because they are programmed to run on the blockchain, these contracts execute exactly how and when they are written without the reliance (or interference) of third-parties. They are not interpreted or enforced by judges, courts, or governments... they are enforced by the Ethereum network.

The Virtual Machine

The core innovation of Ethereum is the EVM or Ethereum Virtual Machine. It is a Turing-complete software running on the Ethereum network, enabling anyone to run whatever program they want, as long as they have the ether to fuel its operation. The EVM simplifies the process of creating blockchain-based applications and makes it more efficient. Rather than needing to build a new blockchain for each application, the EVM enables thousands of different apps to be built on one platform.

Prior to Ethereum, designers and innovators seeking to create new blockchain applications had two choices:

The first was to construct an application on top of Bitcoin. Unfortunately, Bitcoin's scripting language is very limited compared to other languages like C++. While Bitcoin has been modified many times since its inception, attempts to increase the capabilities of its script were either not successful, or not sufficient. The end result is that Bitcoin simply cannot do what some developers want it to do, and attempts to make it more capable are resisted for a variety of reasons.

The other choice was to create your own cryptocurrency. Bitcoin is open-source, making it quite easy for anyone with sufficient skill to take the code and modify it to make something new. This has been done many times, with some of the early altcoins being little more than clones of Bitcoin with slightly different operating parameters. Making a Bitcoin clone for each new application or feature seems like the preferred solution until you realize that each clone needs miners, users, wallets, exchange support, community support... all the things that Bitcoin already has. Reproducing even a fraction of Bitcoin's ecosystem takes time, energy, and money... and success is in no way guaranteed.

Ethereum took an approach that incorporates both potential solutions. Yes, Ethereum is an altcoin. It was a new cryptocurrency that required miners, wallets, etc... everything that Bitcoin already had. BUT, the Ethereum developers wanted to do this work just once. They wanted to create one altcoin with a robust scripting language upon which developers could build whatever they wanted. These new applications wouldn't require their own blockchains, miners, etc., because they'd be using Ethereum's. Now, anyone could develop any application and use the Ethereum system to execute it. All without building their own cryptocurrency from the ground up.

The potential uses of such a framework are boundless. One of the more obvious uses is making digital currencies in only a few dozen lines of code and releasing them on the Ethereum blockchain. This requires a lot less work and a lot less infrastructure than the "hard way" of cloning Bitcoin... and this is exactly what has happened. Later on we'll look at some very ambitious cryptocurrency projects that went this route. For now, just realize that, like "smart contracts," the platform for building other applications is one of the key concepts of Ethereum.

What Can We Use Ethereum For?

Ethereum is primarily intended for developers to use to build and deploy their decentralized applications. Otherwise known as Dapps (for "Decentralized APPlication"), these applications usually serve a very specific purpose... to fill some niche currently dominated by a non-blockchain solution. Bitcoin is a Dapp that provides a P2P digital cash that competes with government-backed "fiat" currency. Because these applications are comprised of code that runs on the blockchain, no one person or entity controls them. Just like Bitcoin is not controlled by the Federal Reserve, the European Union, or the Bank of England... an Ethereum-based Dapp that fills some "contract law" niche would exist outside of the jurisdictions of any nation. Parties not involved in the contract (Lawyers, judges, politicians...) could not alter or impede its operation. Sure, they can seize property or inflict punishment after the fact, but they can't stop the contract from executing as originally written. Now imagine this concept extended to other services like banking, insurance, arbitration, regulatory compliance, or voting. Almost any service that is currently centralized can easily be decentralized with Ethereum... even many services currently provided by governments.

We can also use Ethereum to build DAOs – Decentralized Autonomous Organizations. This is another key concept. These are decentralized organizations that are fully autonomous, having no one leader. They are run purely by networks of smart contracts that have been written on Ethereum. This code replaces the structure and the rules of a traditional organization and eliminates the need for centralized control. Each DAO is owned by those who purchase Ethereum-based tokens that provide the token owner with voting rights. Think of a corporation engaged in a specific line of business... car insurance, for instance. Remove all of the humans from that corporation, and turn all the business rules and contracts (or insurance polices in this example) into smart contracts. That is a DAO. Yes, there are still people involved in some processes, but for the most part those people are just providing inputs (underwriting data) and receiving outputs (insurance claims checks). They are not making decisions. They are not changing (or breaking) procedures. They are not responsible for making sure the company runs according to its rules. Ethereum is doing that.

And because these decentralized applications will run on the blockchain, they will all benefit from the properties of the common to most cryptocurrencies:

Immutable - changes cannot be made to any data by a third party. Transactions cannot be reversed unless that capability is built into the contracts.

Secure – all applications and transactions are secured with cryptography, giving them strong protection against fraud and hacking.

No Downtime – the blockchain is distributed across the network of machines running Ethereum. Apps built upon it can't go down and cannot be switched off... again, unless that capability is built into its design.

The Real Benefits of Ethereum

Think once again back to our insurance company implemented without employees via a DAO. Its operating costs would become significantly smaller than competitors that still relied on flesh-and-blood lawyers and underwriters. But it would still have costs. The cost in Ethereum is called "gas" and it is a universally accepted expense for performing any computational work using the Ethereum. Gas has a consistent cost, regardless of the volatility of Ether's value, helping to stabilize the currency and provide more efficient paths for coding the contracts. In reality, the real value of Ethereum's platform is to create a system in which methodologies can be founded on for running business transactions with more efficient costs and timeframes.

For instance, some vendors (particularly gas stations) have a minimum purchase amount for using a credit card. It might be $5, or $2... or maybe 99cents. Why is that? That amount is directly related to the cost of transferring your account's balance to another account's balance. There is always a net loss of money from any transaction between two parties, because some fees automatically to go to the network in charge of moving that money (such as Visa, Master Card, American Express, etc). This cost becomes prohibitive for micro transactions. It also accumulates quickly as the number of transactions increase. In other words, it costs them more than 99cents to receive 99cents in payment via credit cards. This is as true for cryptocurrencies as it is for traditional money... but the fees are lower, and the currency is infinitely divisible.

Let's clarify look at an example. Currently, it is impossible to pay for streaming video services per the number of seconds you watch. If you were to open a transaction or contract to watch only a second of video and then close the transaction afterward, the resulting payment would be less than one cent. Possibly much less. The US Dollar is not divisible to that amount... but Bitcoin, Ethereum, and most other cryptocurrencies are. There's also the matter of fees, which would completely overwhelm the amount of the transaction itself.

This issue is circumvented with cryptocurrencies. Incredibly small transaction amounts are not a problem, and transaction costs are (or can be) minimized using smart contracts, projects like the Lightning Network, other methods not available in traditional currencies. Compared to Bitcoin, Ethereum is more suited for the infrastructure of businesses and intelligently designed contracts for most business needs and financial transactions. It can be thought of as an alternative to the office building with cubicles. Its infrastructure was especially designed with this in mind, as a "black box" in which to operate transactions and store data.

Chapter 2: A Short History Lesson

Let's take a look at Ethereum's history.

In 2013 a Bitcoin programmer named Vitalik Buterin wanted to expand on the intelligence and decentralized nature of Bitcoin. Part of the problem Mr. Buterin saw with Bitcoin was that it was becoming too centralized. Bitcoin's popularity was growing fast, mainly due to its perceived value as a store of wealth and its potential to supplant systems like Paypal, Visa... and even fiat currencies. What really drew people's attention was the concept of mining.

Mining is the process by which new transactions are written to the blockchain. The process is difficult and becomes even more difficult (requiring more powerful computers) as more people participate. Why would anyone want to? Money. The system rewards successful miners with Bitcoin. Mining was always meant to be a distributed process, but the idea of using a computer to turn electricity into digital gold proved too tempting. As more people poured into the mining ecosystem, it became so difficult that only large groups people with expensive specialized hardware could compete. Solo hobbyists couldn't keep up. Bitcoin mining was now an industry... an industry with few participants, each of which having a large influence over the Bitcoin network. In other words, Bitcoin was becoming centralized. Buterin felt this centralization was contrary to Bitcoin's core goals, and he also felt that Bitcoin could be more useful it was smarter and wasn't focused almost exclusively on one application: replacing cash.

So in March of 2014, Ethereum debuted as a project that could extend blockchain use beyond the traditional peer-to-peer transactions. While legal issues and questions arose to both its legality and technical feasibility, it soon became apparent that it was a legitimate project after Buterin won the "World Technology Award" for the creation of Ethereum.

A major crowdfunding effort for the project began in July of 2014. Investors converted their bitcoin to Ethereum tokens, raising 3,700 BTC (2.3 million USD) on the first day. When crowdfunding ended in September, Buterin and his Ethereum Project had raised $20million from Bitcoin purchases alone.

By the end of May 2016, Ethereum market value quickly rose to more than 1 billion USD. It was quickly becoming a serious contender against Bitcoin itself.

One of the first major projects built on the Ethereum network was a venture capital fund referred to as "The DAO." We already introduced the concept of a Decentralized Autonomous Organization, so the name of this project should be both familiar and confusing. There can be any number of DAOs, but in this case we are referring to a *specific* organization, which simply called itself The DAO.

The DAO comprised the largest bundle of smart contracts on Ethereum and was the earliest, most publicized project on the platform. Its purpose was to collect money from investors and distribute it to projects that the investors voted on... similar to a venture capital firm. The DAO's operation was contained entirely on the Ethereum blockchain. It did not have a street address. It didn't have a Board of Directors. It was not incorporated under the laws of any nation or government. The DAO was just a set of rules and procedures codified in contracts stored in the blockchain. The DAO was so large, in fact, that it was able to raise roughly 170 million dollars in Ethereum tokens from investors.

Unfortunately, there were security flaws in The DAO's smart contracts, which enabled hackers to steal 3.6 million ETH–roughly $50 million at the time–and transfer it to different accounts. So much had been invested and stolen that the Ethereum community was vehement about action being taken. There were contentious debates about two options: a soft fork, wherein the pilfered currency would be "burned" or made unusable by either the thieves or the original owners, and a hard fork or a total rollback of the blockchain to a point before the exploit occurred, resulting in a kind of alternate timeline. A soft fork would maintain the blockchain in its original form, complete with The DAO's creation and the multi-million-dollar exploit. A hard fork would go back in time and create a new reality where the DAO exploit never happened.

Vitalik and the other Ethereum developers favored a hard fork which was the action eventually taken. However, many

Ethereum users disagreed with this decision, as they believed in the concept of the blockchain being immutable and permanent. As a result, they created a version of Ethereum on the unaltered blockchain, which they called Ethereum Classic (ETC). Although the two versions of Ethereum share a common beginning, there are incompatible with each other.

Ethereum Classic is still a major cryptocurrency and, while it lags behind Bitcoin, Ethereum and Litecoin in value, it is still in the top 10 in terms of market capitalization (as of the time of writing).

Despite this early drama, Ethereum remains one of the most technologically innovative forms of cryptocurrency and shows no signs of slowing down. Some day, a cryptocurrency may overtake Bitcoin and Ethereum just might be the one to do it.

Chapter 3: A Currency for the Future

Now you have an understanding of what Ethereum is and where it came from... what can it do? What applications are being developed that make it worth investing time and money into? Currently, the majority of the use cases involve transmitting financial data. Many of the Ethereum apps that are in development, however, are going to expand the blockchain paradigm significantly.

Here's a look at the Ethereum application ecosystem as of 2017:

Blockstream

Blockstream is a company working on a variety of projects. The most important of these is increasing the speed of cryptocurrency based projects that work with smart contracts. The company recently saw an influx of more than $50 million during a round of funding. Those funds are being put to work enhancing protocol strength and funding the completion of several projects including the Lightning Network, which will help speed up smaller blockchain transactions and make everyday usage of cryptocurrencies more likely. The Lightning Network received a lot of attention in 2017 as a potential solution to Bitcoin's scaling problems.

Aeternity

Similar to Blockstream, Aeternity is another project attempting to make it easier for Ethereum to grow larger and faster. It is striving to generate a network that would handle all the smart contracts separately from the primary blockchain functions, increasing transaction speeds in the process. The contracts that use this secondary network would only come into contact with the primary blockchain at points where verification of transactions was required.

ContentKid

ContentKid is a unique way of using the blockchain to access streaming content. ContentKid works by purchasing subscription time to various services such as Hulu or Netflix and then renting out the time in short bursts to interested consumers. This allows users legal access to a wide variety of content in daily or even hourly bursts rather than in via a traditional monthly or yearly model. The technology behind it provides users with access as needed by automatically completing transactions based on time spent watching content.

Blockphase

Blockphase is a blockchain based tool that helps combat copyright infringement in augmented reality, 360-degree video, and virtual reality content. Users are able to add their content to the Blockphase blockchain, which then searches the internet for instances of infringement. This allows users to store and manage their copyrights more easily and decreases the likelihood of intellectual theft, freeing them to create as opposed to having to protect their work.

Starting Your Own Cryptocurrency.

Most cryptocurrencies in existence today are clones of the original bitcoin idea, some using the exact same code. As discussed in a previous chapter, each coin has its own separate blockchain, which must be supported by miners, wallets, etc. But what if, instead of creating entirely new blockchain networks for yet more cryptocurrencies, we could use the existing Ethereum platform with its infrastructure already in place?

That is exactly what is happening now.

Numerous currencies... each with their own niches and objectives... have been built upon Ethereum. Depending on the creativity of the developer, these custom currencies can represent a portion of equity in a company, a quantity of a real-life asset, or a portion of profits of a Dapp on the Ethereum blockchain. The possibilities are endless.

Here are some examples:
BitNation (PAT)- A proof-of-concept cyber-government that contains blockchain-based solutions for insurance, education, ID cards, and diplomacy programs like ambassadors, refugees, etc. Bitnation.co
Ethlance - A freelancer platform where workers are paid with Ether. ethlance.com
Swarm City (SWT) - A decentralized P2P sharing economy. Users are required to have a Swarm City Token to do transactions in their ecosystem. Www.swarm.city
Civic (CVC)- Decentralized identity verification via the blockchain. www.civic.com
FunFair (FUN) - a platform for online casinos and gambling. funfair.io
WINGS - a platform for blockchain-based crowdfunding. www.wings.ai

Edgeless (EDG) - another platform for online gambling. edgeless.io

Basic Attention Token (BAT) - blockchain-based digital advertising. basicattentiontoken.org

Metal (MTL) - an end-user digital currency that rewards people for spending it. metalpay.com

Acebusters (NZT) - is a poker platform based on the blockchain. acebusters.com

0x (ZRX) - (pronounced "ZERO-X") a protocol enabling the effortless exchange of Ethereum-based assets. 0xproject.com

1World Online (1WO) - Another advertising platform, this one focusing on interactive media and audience engagement. welcome.1worldonline.com

8 Circuit Studios (8BT) - a gaming platform that uses the blockchain to track ownership of virtual goods. 8circuitstudios.com

HireMatch (HRC) - a blockchain-based employment service. hirematch.io

Kencoin (KCN) - an anonymous currency for transactions related to sex and dating. kencoin.org

Hubii (HBT) - A decentralized content network. www.hubii.network

Storj (SJCX) - a decentralized cloud storage plaftform. Www.storj.io

This list goes on. Literally. There are over 340 Ethereum-based tokens in various stages of fund-raising, and the list grows daily.

Each of these projects and their corresponding tokens have (or will have) a dollar value and will also add value to the Ethereum platform upon which they were built. Any of them could be the next Microsoft, or Steam, or YouTube, or State Farm.

However, please note that the legality of some tokens, particularly those involving gambling or ownership of a company, are still murky. Investors in high regulation environments (i.e. the United States) should be wary. *This list is not intended to be a recommendation to buy, sell, or otherwise become involved in anything.*

Future uses

Beyond the projects already underway, Ethereum has the potential to expand into the following areas:

Law

Smart contracts are already making their way into the legal arena in conjunction with traditional contracts. They make it easier to enact all the "legalese" in typical contracts related to the timing and specifics of certain actions. Smart contracts cut through all the red tape and automate things that need to happen once certain external factors are met. In theory, if this practice continues to become more common, there will be less a need for this type of boilerplate content in contracts. It could all be handled automatically in the Ethereum blockchain.

Financial services

The financial service industry is already taking steps to make Ethereum a part of its infrastructure. The Enterprise Ethereum Alliance is racing towards a scenario where the Ethereum platform houses a secondary blockchain tailored to the needs of the financial sectors. Additionally, smart contracts are going to continue to see an increased usage managing trade clearing and the generation of settlements. Smart contracts can also be used to determine coupon payments and in the generation of bonds at the point of expiration.

Smart contracts are also starting to pop up in the settlement of insurance claims. With additional refinement, this type of smart contract would be able to take insurance adjusters out of the system completely. The need for humans would be minimized further as smart cars become able to relay data directly to the insurance company. Insurers would also be able to increase or decrease rates automatically based on predetermined driver statistics. Remember the thought exercise earlier where we removed the humans from an insurance company and called it a DAO? We're only a few years away from that being reality.

Healthcare

Ethereum isn't going to cure cancer, but smart contracts are already helping patients and their data stay connected. Preliminary usage results from hospital testing indicates that linking patients and their charts through a blockchain would decrease the likelihood of clerical errors by as much as 40 percent.

Apps are currently in development that will connect individuals to their health information automatically based on social security numbers. This would mean no more transferring medical records from one doctor to another, or having to track down old x-rays or test results. Everything would be readily available at the press of a button.

The Ethereum platform is also being put to use tracking medical studies. Study participants are having their data transferred automatically for collection. If they are being paid for participation, those payments could happen automatically (via smart contract) when the study comes to an end. Perhaps unsurprisingly, a version of this same technology is on its way to a variety of personal internet devices such as those that track physical activity and fitness goals.

Electric vehicles

Tesla is allegedly working with the Ethereum platform to develop a blockchain-based method of charging electric cars. Owners of electric vehicles would pull up to charging stations and plug in without having to enter payment or identification information. Each car would be linked to a specific smart contract that would, in turn, be linked to a bank account.

Shipping

Work is already being done to put smart contracts to work updating and correlating clerical information. The technology is poised to revolutionize the shipping industry. Supply chain movement will soon be clearly visible in a blockchain that is automatically updated as products move from place to place. Payment will also be handled through the blockchain after products reach a predetermined location. The same process will handle bills of lading, credit and promise payments. As the usage among manufactures grows, the history of every product that you receive will grower longer and more detailed until you are able to track the path everything took from the manufacturer straight to your doorstep.

Chapter 4: How to Buy Ethereum

Disclaimer: *I am not a financial or investment adviser. This chapter is general advice only. It has been prepared without taking into account your objectives, financial situation or needs. Before acting on this advice you should consider its appropriateness in regard to your own objectives, financial situation and needs.*

We've talked a lot about features, ongoing projects and future use cases, but we have barely mentioned the Ethereum currency, ether. This is intentional. Recall from the introduction that the focus and purpose of Ethereum is its intelligent scripting capabilities... not its currency. Ether is a vital but secondary part of the Ethereum architecture. But that doesn't mean we should ignore it entirely. In fact, given the price behavior over the past year, Ethereum's currency is something that everyone should be paying a lot more attention to. According to market capitalization, Ethereum is the second largest Cryptocurrency and has the potential overtake Bitcoin. The value of ether has grown at a nearly exponential rate, and it is likely to continue as more ambitious projects built atop the Ethereum platform. in A little ether now could turn into a life-changing amount of money in just a few years... just like Bitcoin.

So how does one actually buy ether?

Creating an account on the exchange

As with any other cryptocurrencies, Ethereum needs to be bought and sold via exchanges. There are many trading platforms. The most popular options include Coinbase (coinbase.com), Gemini (gemini.com), and Bittrex (bittrex.com). Of these three, Coinbase is without a doubt the most newbie-friendly; If you have little or no experience with Bitcoin or Ethereum, I suggest you start there.

Verifying the account

Most exchanges will need to verify your identity before doing much (or any) business with you. New users are frequently required to upload images of identifying documents such as driver's licenses, passports, or utility bills to verify identity and citizenship. After providing documentation, verification can another day or two, depending on how popular the exchange is. Some exchanges won't let you trade at all until you verify your identity while others may limit you to very small amounts. So don't expect to open an account today and buy thousands of dollars in ETH (or any other altcoin). Plan ahead and adjust your expectations.

Depositing currency

If you are trying to buy ETH with dollars (or other fiat currency) the next step would be to deposit that currency into the account. Setting up the connection between the exchange and your bank may be instantaneous... or it may take a few days, depending on the exchange. Once done, it may (or may not) take a day or two for the money to transfer. This entire process may strike some as frustrating and slow... and if it does, recall that this is one of the reasons cryptocurrencies were created in the first place. The roadblocks here are due to the traditional banks and their systems, not with the exchanges.

Speaking of which, you are not limited to buying ETH with dollars. If you already have bitcoin, you can deposit BTC and exchange it for ETH almost instantly (well... in an hour or so). Even better, you can skip creating an account an exchange entirely. How? Use the Coinomi wallet (coinomi.com) on your Android phone or tablet to convert not only between BTC and ETH, but between any of their *many* supported altcoins. Just transfer some BTC into the wallet, use the "exchange" menu option, and select Ethereum as your destination currency. Coinomi uses a service called Shapeshift to execute the exchange. You can use Shapeshift directly (without Coinomi) by going to their website at shapeshift.io. There is not currently an iOS version of the Coinomi wallet, so for Apple fans, the Shapeshift website may be the only option for exchange-less purchases.

Start trading

When your account is verified and money has been deposited, you can start buying or selling ether and other cryptocurrencies. The interface of each exchange is different, and you need to have some patience not only for learning the interface, but for the purchases to be performed once you place the order.

Withdraw the ether into a wallet

Once you have purchased ETH, the next step is to withdraw it into a wallet that is under your control. This is a step that most people... especially new users... skip. They shouldn't. Bitcoin has a long and disturbing history of people getting their BTC stolen from exchanges that were hacked or that turned out to be fraudulent. This isn't implying that cryptocurrency is insecure... but it is implying that cryptocurrency exchanges should not be trusted to store your currency one second longer than it takes to make the exchange. Even popular and trusted exchanges like Coinbase should be used only for converting currency, never for storage. People once regarded MtGox with the same trust they put in Coinbase. They regretted it.

You will need to store your ether in a safe place. Install and use a wallet that supports Ethereum. Wallets are discussed further in the next chapter. For now, recognize and remember the need to use one. Leaving purchases on an exchange should never be your default... this is akin to buying gold jewelry on Amazon and having them store it for you in their warehouse. It takes just a few minutes to find and set up an Ethereum wallet, and if you opted to use Coinomi to make your bitcoin-To-ether exchange, you're already good to go (hint-hint).

Dealing with volatility

It is quite reasonable for markets to suffer price fluctuations, or volatility. Some markets are more volatile than others, particularly commodities and currencies. This is natural. The market for cryptocurrencies is orders of magnitude more volatile than what even experienced investors are comfortable with. High transaction speeds, low transaction costs, and the tendency for the internet to over-react to... well... everything... produces short and medium term price swings that are absolutely awe-inspiring. Dealing with volatility is quite simple. You will just need to get your emotions under control and keep a calm mind. Have a plan and Act. Do not React.

Here is the plan: You should hold Ethereum on a long-term basis. You need to understand that cryptocurrencies... particularly Ethereum... have great potential that hasn't been tapped yet. This potential is what you are investing in. The short and medium-term fluctuations, while they can be frightening and profitable, are largely driven by factors that have nothing to do with that potential. Unless there is a fundamental change in Ethereum that makes it somehow less able to reach its potential... ignore the price volatility and hold. Or, to borrow from Bitcoin terminology: HODL.

Chapter 5: How to Use Ethereum

You will need a secure place for storing your ether and creating transactions. This place is an Ethereum wallet running on a device that you control. The device can be a phone, tablet, desktop computer... or even a piece of paper.

Desktop wallets

The official Ethereum wallet is called Mist, and can be found at https://github.com/ethereum/mist/releases. However, being "official" doesn't necessarily make it better than other options. There are in fact several desktop clients to choose from, and my personal recommendation is not to use any of them. If you're dealing with small amounts of ether, use a mobile wallet instead (see next section). If you're stockpiling investment-level amounts of ether, then skip the desktop entirely and use either a hardware wallet or a paper wallet. Both are discussed below.

Why skip the desktop? There is nothing inherently wrong with any of the available wallets, but most people have a false sense of security when it comes to their own machines. The desktop is a HUGE target for hackers, and yours isn't nearly as secure as you think it is. Most people also use their one desktop for everything from online banking to watching porn. Some of these activities make them even more of a target... and even easier to hack. Unless you have a machine that is devoted to the sole purpose of storing cryptocurrency and is kept offline when not in use... skip the desktop.

Mobile wallets

Mobile wallets run on your phone or tablet. They may not have as many features as a full desktop client, but they are easy to use and definitely newbie friendly. Android has numerous cryptocurrency wallets to choose from. Apple iOS has significantly fewer.

Are these wallets any safer than a desktop wallet? Not really. I recommend them over desktop wallets for three reasons. I've already mentioned the first: they are much easier to use. Better user interfaces, fewer advanced features to trip over, and the ability to use a camera to read QR codes make them a clear choice for new users.

The second reason is that people tend to think of their desktop as secure and are thus tempted to store large amounts of cryptocurrency on them. Then they go surf the internet, pick up a keylogger or a trojan, and the next time they access their Ethereum wallet, their fortune disappears. While this sequence of events can happen on a tablet, it is less likely and, more importantly, people aren't tempted to store their life's savings on a cellphone.

Finally, people are much more likely to have an old cellphone sitting around than they are a laptop or desktop. Why is this important? That old phone or tablet can easily be converted into dedicated cryptocurrency device that is kept offline when not in use... which will be most of the time.. This makes it almost (but not quite) as good as a hardware wallet.

Hardware wallets

These are small devices that look like fancy USB thumb drives. What they are inside, though, is magic. They have the ability to turn even a known insecure computer into a bulletproof cryptocurrency wallet. All the cryptocurrency operations happen in an encrypted space on the device, invisible to the computer it is plugged into. The two front runners in hardware wallets are Trezor (trezor.io) and Ledger (ledgerwallet.com). Both were originally designed for Bitcoin, but both can be used for Ethereum as well. Hardware wallets cost between $60 and $100 USD, depending on which model you buy and how diligent you are in searching for bargains. This is a lot of money for a device to store pocket change, but if need a place to park thousands of dollars worth of ether, you should strongly consider buying one.

Paper wallets

A paper wallet is a piece of paper (or plastic or metal) with an Ethereum address written on it, along with the code used to access the currency.

We didn't go into the details of how cryptocurrencies work, so it may not be obvious that a Bitcoin or Ethereum address can receive funds even if the wallet that contains the address is offline... but they can. The transactions are stored on the blockchain, not in the wallet. When you open your wallet software, it scans the blockchain for changes to the addresses it controls. Not only that, but if you give your wallet software the secret code (called a "private key") to an Ethereum address that it didn't previously know about, it will then be able to import funds and make transactions with that address.

If you combine these two revelations... that addresses can receive funds when not online and that they can be imported to wallets... you have an understanding of how paper wallets work. You can send ether to the address on the paper wallet without fear that its associated computer will be hacked because there is no associated computer. When you need to spend the funds, most wallets will allow you to import the paper wallet address and transfer its contents. This takes only a few seconds and is a lot less complicated than it sounds.

Which Wallet?!

If you've read this far expecting to find a recommendation for an Ethereum wallet, I won't disappoint you. But instead of recommending one wallet for iOS and another for Android and yet another for Windows, I'll give you one name that works everywhere. Jaxx (jaxx.io) produces wallets on multiple platforms that support multiple cryptocurrencies, including Ethereum. It isn't the absolute best wallet, nor is it the one that I personally use, but it is secure and simple enough to recommend to new users.

...and if you absolutely must know what I use for Ethereum: I have a hardware wallet from Ledger and I use the previously mentioned Coinomi wallet on Android. The absolute best cryptocurrency wallet on Android is, in my opinion, Mycelium (wallet.mycelium.com). Unfortunately it does not support Ethereum.

You are the Bank

Regardless of the type of wallet, make sure you remember your passcode and/or wallet recovery phrase. In the case of a paper wallet these are printed on the page which you MUST NEVER LOSE. These passcodes or phrases represent the private keys to your encrypted Ethereum wallet. Losing your private key isn't the same as forgetting the password to your Twitter account. There is no reset. There is no tech support. Without the password, you are permanently locked out of wallet with *zero* chance of recovering your money. If this makes you uneasy... good. That means you're paying attention. Getting rid of banks and other third parties means you are now the bank, and the job of securing your money is 100% yours.

Chapter 6: Ethereum Mining

Note: I include this chapter on mining for completeness, not because I recommend mining as a profitable or fulfilling venture for new users. It isn't. Mining Ethereum for profit isn't something most new users will be able to do without a moderate amount of startup capital, free or cheap electricity, and a high tolerance for frustration. If you are seeking profit, instead consider just buying ETH and holding it as the price rises. If the idea of literally creating money with your computer is too much of an appeal to pass up, then here are the basic concepts.

Mining is the use of computers to perform difficult calculations in a race to decide who gets to write the next block of transactions to the blockchain. The calculations get harder as the number of participants increases. The "winner" gets rewarded in cryptocurrency, and the next race starts immediately after the previous one finishes. That is the shortest explanation of cryptocurrency mining you will ever read.

Solo mining: This when you mine by yourself. The advantage of this is that any mining rewards you obtain are yours to keep. You don't have to share. Unfortunately, mining is difficult, and the likelihood of a solo miner earning a reward is minuscule.

Pool Mining: - With pool mining many miners join forces to try to earn the reward. The resulting currency is then distributed between the minors, usually based on their level of participation. Miners typically pay a small fee to the pool operator for maintaining the service.

Solo miners make money slowly and infrequently. They profit through luck and patience. Pool miners make smaller amounts of money, but they make it more often. They profit by keeping their machines running.

In exchange for mining on the Ethereum platform, miners receive ether to offset their costs and hopefully turn a profit. They also receive a portion of the transaction fees that are charged to users of Ethereum. The value of ether is currently a little over $300, but it changes rapidly... meaning the profitability of ETH mining (measured in USD) fluctuates. A miner may go from making a healthy profit to losing money and then back to profitable again in a matter of days. Worse still, since the mining difficultly is almost always increasing, the machines they use to mine eth become obsolete (I.e. unprofitable) over time.

Getting Started

Finding "the best mining hardware" is a bit like finding "the best computer". It is a rapidly moving target. Hardware manufactures are in a perpetual race to keep up with mining difficulty. Trailing far, far behind both of these things is you and your wallet. The most powerful machine this year may be far out of your price range, and it may also be obsolete next year.

The best place to go for up-to-date information is going to be the Ethereum Mining subreddit at https://www.reddit.com/r/EtherMining/. You should easily be able to find out the current state of the market as well as what hardware is currently considered state of the art. A variety of mining machines can be found on Amazon.com, but that may not be the best place to buy them. Instead of going to a specific retailer and seeing what they have available, find out what you want to buy first, and then search for it on the internet. Don't forget Ebay. Miners will often sell older but still profitable machines to pay for the newer ones.

Regardless of the type of system you choose to go with, you are going to need dedicated hardware in order to mine effectively. While technically you may be able to mine using your computer's video card or your laptop's CPU, specialized mining machines are always going to outpace you. The most popular chips in these machines are made by ASIC and are generally about 100 times faster than a high-end gaming computer. Trying to mine without having the right hardware in place will generally just end up costing you more time and money than the entire endeavor is worth.

Also, remember that these mining rigs... be they overpowered graphics cards or something else... usually need to be connected to a computer and provided with power. Lots of power. Some mining rigs take their power from the computer they're plugged into, which means that computer must have a very strong power supply to support the multiple-mining-rig setups that the pros use. Rigs that have their own power supplies are more expensive, and they still need to be plugged into something to access the internet. This means they may slow down the computer, making it frustrating to use that computer for other tasks. In other words: you might need to buy a new computer or upgrade an old one if you mine at anything other than hobbyist levels.

Getting Online

After you have a mining machine ready, you will need to download the program that you will use to automate the mining process. There are several versions of this type of program available, the most commonly used ones are BFGminer, EasyMiner and CGminer. EasyMiner is the only one that uses a standard graphical interface, the others run via command line prompts. While I don't recommend mining to new cryptocurrency users, EasyMiner is the software they should use if they insist on giving it a shot.

Connecting to a Pool

Once you have the required software and hardware, the next thing you will need to do is to join an ether mining pool. A mining pool is a confederation of miners who band together with the goal of verifying blocks more quickly than they can each do alone. The rewards for doing so are then shared among the miners who helped with the verification. While joining a pool is optional, the amount of computer power required for profitable mining is far what most solo machines can do in a reasonable period.

If you decide to strike out on your own, then you will need to download the Ethereum core client to keep your machine in sync with the Ethereum blockchain. This client can be downloaded from Ethereum.org. Assuming you decide to go with a mining pool instead, then all you will need to do is follow the instructions of the leader of the pool instead.

There are many pools to choose from, each with slightly different rules, fees, and payment schedules. Don't obsess over choosing the perfect one right now. If you're just getting started pick Ethermine (ethermine.org), F2Pool (f2pool.com), or DwarfPool (dwarfpool.com). These are the first, second, and third largest mining pools, respectively. If you can't mine profitably with one of these, picking a smaller pool with different fees won't fix it. Once you know what you're doing, then consider switching pools to earn a fraction of a percent more profit... maybe. Joining up with an extremely popular pool (like the three I listed) means that you will have the chance to get in on more rewards. Going with a smaller pool means that your individual shares from each reward are likely going to be larger. There is a balance point that requires trial-and-error and research to find... but that isn't what you need to be worrying about on your first week mining.

Cloud Mining

It is possible to mine ether using servers hosted on platforms such as AWS (aws.amazon.com) or digitalocean (digitalocean.com). However, this is even less newbie-friendly than buying hardware and the profitability is unproven. Don't waste your time.

There are also Ethereum mining contracts such as those by Genesis Mining (genesis-mining.com). These companies provide you with your own dedicated mining rig hosted in their data center. I advise even experienced people to avoid mining contracts. While Genesis Mining is a reputable company, cloud mining contracts in general tend to be unprofitable. Any profits seen are generally derived from the increase in value of ether, and can be obtained by simply taking the money you would spend on a mining contract and buying ETH on an exchange.

Chapter 7: Three Rules

The moment bitcoin obtained a monetary value, hackers and con-men came out of the woodwork to relieve unsuspecting victims of their BTC. Early adopters navigated a minefield of scams and hacks; every lesson they learned was at the expense of someone losing their bitcoin, often in amounts that would have made them multi-millionaires today. The situation is much better now, but those early lessons still apply, not just to Bitcoin, but to its descendants as well. Fortunately, you don't have to learn those lessons the hard way. Most of the heartache (not to mention bankruptcies) of previous years can be avoided by following my Three Simple Rules for Cryptocurrency.

Avoid web-based wallets. Regard any service that offers to hold your cryptocurrency for you with suspicion. The entire point of Bitcoin (and, by extension, all cryptocurrencies) was to give people direct control of their wealth, eliminating the need for 3rd parties like banks or credit card companies. Using a hosted wallet may sound convenient, but it violates this core principle of cryptocurrency. It is also unnecessary, risky, and not very smart. Using a web wallet is the internet equivalent of giving all the cash in your wallet to a well-dressed stranger who offers to hold it for you. There is no such thing as a "cryptocurrency savings account." There are no "Ethereum banks." Anyone trying to convince you otherwise is suspect. Yes, they may be trying to market a legitimate new, though unnecessary, service. They may also be trying to scam you. You won't be able to tell the difference until it is too late. This rule also applies to online exchanges. As mentioned before, you shouldn't leave currency in an online exchange unless you are intending to trade it in the very near future. The "very near future" is measured in hours, not days or weeks. I cannot emphasize this enough... trusting strangers on the internet to hold money resulted in lost fortunes and ruined lives. I use the Coinbase exchange quite often and recommend that company to new users all the time. I Do Not Trust Them To Hold My Money.

Don't store life-changing amounts of cryptocurrency on a phone, tablet, or computer. Ether, bitcoin, and other cryptocurrencies are incredibly secure. But this security does not extend into whatever computer or mobile device you use. Bitcoin doesn't make your computer hack-proof. Ethereum doesn't make your phone incapable of being stolen. You must understand and appreciate the difference between having a secure application (an Ethereum wallet) and having a secure platform (your phone). Do not store large amounts of currency on insecure platforms. Your desktop, phone, and tablet are inherently insecure and shouldn't be used to store amounts of cryptocurrency that would bankrupt you or cause you to miss mortgage payments if lost. Mobile devices are for "petty cash" amounts... money that you spend in a day or a week. For savings account or investment-level amounts, use specialized secure hardware wallets like Trezor (trezor.io) or Ledger (ledgerwallet.com), or use paper wallets. Remember: With cryptocurrency, you are the bank. Your bank doesn't store your retirement account on a phone, so neither should you.

Don't skip the backups. Most wallets offer a capability to back up your private keys, usually as a string of random words or phrases that you must write down and keep safe. This backup process is simple, but it is awkward and some people choose to ignore it. If your wallet offers a private key backup and doesn't FORCE you to use it... use it anyway. This list of random words is how you will transfer your cryptocurrency to your new wallet if your old one gets damaged or stolen. Think of it this way: suppose you kept your life's savings in a safe inside your house. Now imagine your house catches fire. The password you use to access your wallet is like the combination to the safe. The private key is like a science-fiction teleporter that can transport the safe from your burning house to a brand new one on the other side of town. You might use your passcode every day, but the private key is something you may never need... but if you ever do need it, you will deeply regret not having it. It should go without saying that these backups (usually written on paper) should be kept safe. Keep them in a real, physical safe if you have one. I'm not a fan of storing them a bank's safe deposit box, because you are once again putting a 3rd party in control of your money. But if that doesn't bother you... do it. It's better than leaving your private keys on a notepad beside your computer

Side note: the very idea that you can "back up" your savings and restore it somewhere else via the internet is, in technical terms: Incredibly Awesome.

That's it. You'd think there would be more and, in truth, there is. But the above simple rules represent the biggest mistakes that cryptocurrency users make. They are the answers to questions that new users either ask... or wish they had. Each rule has multiple stories behind it. Very few of those stories have a happy ending. Almost none of them do. Literal fortunes have been lost because people purchased cryptocurrency and were unwilling or unable to take the steps necessary to secure it. As stated before, with cryptocurrency you are the bank. If you cannot do what banks do (hold money securely) then you should keep your cryptocurrency holdings to hobbyist or "petty cash" amounts. I'm assuming that additional guidelines such as "investigate things before you invest in them" and "if something seems too good to be true, it probably is" are obvious and don't need to be stated here, but they apply to cryptocurrency as much, or more, than they do everywhere else.

Conclusion and Further Reading

You've reached the end of Ethereum: A Primer. Thank you for reading.

I've tried to make this book short and interesting, yet still valuable as an introduction to Ethereum. With a topic as complex as cryptocurrency, a certain amount of techno-speak is unavoidable. I've endeavored to keep it to a minimum, but my efforts to do so may have left this book lacking in some of the deeper technical areas. For that reason, I'm going to provide some links to additional resources that you can use to take your understanding of Ethereum to the next level.

But first, let's recap what you've learned already:

What Ethereum Is: A more intelligent and developer friendly version of Bitcoin AND a platform upon which applications can be built.
What Ethereum Is Not: Another end-user currency for buying things on and off the internet.

Why Ethereum is Exciting: It lowers the bar for innovation AND enables much more complex transactions.

You've been introduced to the concepts of ***Smart Contracts*** (contracts enforced by the Ethereum blockchain rather than by courts and governments) and ***Distributed Autonomous Organizations*** (blockchain-based corporations with little to no physical presence).

You've seen some exciting projects already underway to bring everything from cloud storage (Storj) to identity verification (Civic) onto the Ethereum blockchain.

You've learned the basic steps for buying and holding ether, the Ethereum currency. You even know to get started mining ether should you chose to do so.

And finally, you've learned my Three Simple Rules for Cryptocurrency, which can be humorously paraphrased as: ***Trust No One; Not even Your Computer; Always Have a Backup.*** A more serious summary would be ***Don't Buy What You Can't Protect***.

Hopefully all of that sounds familiar. If so, then my purpose for writing this book has been met. If you want more, then consider the following links as additional homework:

The Ethereum homepage (ethereum.org) will try to sell you on the features and benefits of Ethereum, but doesn't go out of its way to be friendly to the less technical. Be sure to check out the forum at forum.ethereum.org.

The Ethereum subreddit (reddit.com/r/ethereum/) is an excellent place to keep up to date on Ethereum developments. Like the main website, it assumes a basic level of knowledge that you should already have from this book.

Coindesk's *What Is Ethereum* page (coindesk.com/information/what-is-ethereum/) and Ethereum 101 (ethereum101.org) take everything back down to the basics. If you need a refresher, this is a good one.

On the opposite extreme, the Ethereum White Paper (github.com/ethereum/wiki/wiki/White-Paper) contains all the deeply technical "how's" and "why's" that make most people's eyes gloss over. If you intend to go beyond investing or mining and become a developer or entrepreneur... you should read and understand this paper. Twice.

There is no shortage of cryptocurrency videos on Youtube. Unfortunately, very few of them are specific to Ethereum, and almost none are intended for people brand new to the platform. Nevertheless, Ethereum has an official channel at www.youtube.com/user/ethereumproject. Most of the videos there are technical in nature. Ethereum's creator, Vitalik Buterin, is no stranger to Youtube. Of all biographies, interviews, and technical talks featuring Buterin, my favorite is also one of the most recent: Decentralizing Everything is a TechCrunch interview at bit.ly/TCBUTERIN. There you can watch Buterin explain in his own words what Ethereum is and why it is important. I highly recommend it.

And finally, EthList is a crowd-sourced Ethereum reading list that can take you from "What is Ethereum" to creating your own distributed applications. This list of resources is very long, very comprehensive, and updated often. You can find it at github.com/Scanate/EthList.

These pages, plus the various links they contain, are more than enough to satisfy your thirst for Ethereum. Whether your Ethereum education continues or ends here, I want to say once again:

Thanks For Reading.

Sincerely,
Eric Morse

www.ingramcontent.com/pod-product-compliance
Lightning Source LLC
Chambersburg PA
CBHW071221240526
45470CB00018B/2098